A Guide to the Characteristics of the Successful Entrepreneur

Louis Callaghan-Inge

A Guide to the Characteristics of the Successful Entrepreneur

First published in 2020.
Copyright © Louis Callaghan-Inge 2020
Louis Callaghan-Inge has asserted his right as the identified author of this work and this is in accordance with the Copyright, Designs and Patents Act 1988.
Cover design copyright © Louis Callaghan-Inge
All rights reserved. No part of this publication may be reproduced, stored in a retrieval system, or transmitted in any form by any means, electronic, mechanical, photocopying, recording, or otherwise, without the prior permission of the copyright owner.

ISBN 9798566272030

Louis Callaghan-Inge

About the author

Louis Callaghan-Inge is a 17-year-old student at Oakwood Park Grammar School in Maidstone, Kent, studying Economics, French and PE. After being amazed by the street food of Hong Kong during a family holiday in 2016, he started his own business named 'The Bubble Waffle Company'. He has since appeared on various news channels and radio stations, including BBC South East News, KMTV and Heart radio.
His interest in all things business led him to write this guide. This book has been written as his EPQ project.

A Guide to the Characteristics of the Successful Entrepreneur

Contents

Introduction
10

What does success mean to an entrepreneur?
19

How do entrepreneurs gain the characteristics which lead them to success?
29

How have the characteristics of the successful entrepreneur changed over time?
45

Which are the three most important characteristics of the successful entrepreneur?
65

Conclusion
79

In this book, I will provide you with a short guide into the characteristics you will need to become a successful entrepreneur, based on similarities between successful entrepreneurs within a variety of industries and time periods.

I hope that by reading this book, it will enable you to implement these characteristics into your own personality to give you the best chance of becoming a successful entrepreneur. Instead of years of trial and error, using these characteristics will fast-track your entrepreneurial journey and let you reach success quicker.

Introduction

"Bill and I were very different characters" – Bill Gates that is. This is how Richard Branson described Bill Gates after a day of sailing and tennis on his private Caribbean island. Two of the wealthiest, most powerful and most influential entrepreneurs in recent history supposedly have completely different characteristics? But surely all successful entrepreneurs have things in common, surely there must be common traits they share which have been crucial for their success. Perhaps a special attribute that enables them to persuade with a smile or make money from nothing.

As an entrepreneur myself, the make-up of a successful entrepreneur has intrigued me for years. In 2016 aged 13, I was on a family holiday in Hong Kong. As interesting as the famous skyline and giant statues of Buddha were, I was fascinated by the hundreds of bustling street-food stalls which littered every alley and street corner, overwhelmed by jostling and disorganised crowds of hungry locals. I happened to repeatedly come across stalls selling a certain sweet treat, which involved a pale yellow-coloured batter being poured into a hot mould with rows of spherical dimples inside, before the iron was closed and flipped. Without a timer, the chef knew exactly when to re-open the lid, revealing something I had never seen before, something they called a 'Bubble Waffle'.

I returned home from holiday charged with excitement and with the desire to show people in England what they had been missing! I have always had a deep interest in the world of business and how it functioned, so I thought I could put this passion into practise by setting up my very own stall selling these bubble waffles. After the process of convincing and getting permission from my parents, I set about putting together a plan to set up the business. Once I had assembled a worn-out gazebo and some tables from the garden, bought a second hand 'bubble waffle' machine online, received a health and hygiene certificate and countless hours perfecting the recipe, we set off for our first event.

Four years later the business is doing very well, with three employees, a branded gazebo and four brand new waffle machines. I consider myself an entrepreneur by definition, however it is not a full-time occupation, not to the extent where I am relying on my business to pay rent or bills, and by no means am I close to owning a Ferrari! However, I feel I have learnt enough in the last four years to understand the basic principles of entrepreneurship and business. These last four years have only amplified my interest into entrepreneurship, and I am more eager than ever to understand the characteristics and traits common among successful entrepreneurs. My research into the topic will hopefully provide both me and you as the reader invaluable information to use in our own future ventures.

A Guide to the Characteristics of the Successful Entrepreneur

What separates a successful entrepreneur from an unsuccessful one is the way they think, behave and act, which is all determined by their characteristics. This book will provide you with the understanding of the most important characteristics of a successful entrepreneur and to refine my research, I decided to try and specifically find the three most important characteristics. This way I will be able to compare many important characteristics of successful entrepreneurs, to hopefully reach a more justifiable conclusion. As well as granting you with the answer to the most important characteristics of the successful entrepreneur, this book will provide you with general information regarding the characteristics of a successful entrepreneur.

The book will be structured into four sections. The first two will look at which point does an entrepreneur considers themselves to be successful and examine how the characteristics which have led them to success are acquired. The penultimate section will discuss how the characteristics of a successful entrepreneur have changed over time, and the last section will look at the characteristics themselves which I have concluded to be the most important, explaining why each one is so significant and the benefit it can provide when implemented into your entrepreneurial life.

It is important to understand the reasoning behind why I have chosen certain characteristics over others. The characteristics I have chosen as the three most important are not just those I saw most frequently during my research. I believe frequency is most definitely a factor when determining the most important characteristics, however it is not conclusive. For example, if I have come across a certain quality common between many of the entrepreneurs I have researched, it is definitely important, but the same entrepreneurs may value other attributes to be more influential in their success. The three characteristics that I have chosen are simply the ones I believe are the most important in achieving success as an entrepreneur.

I have used a range of research to provide reference for this book. As well as using my own experience as an entrepreneur, I have interviewed entrepreneurs local to Kent who I consider to be successful. The first of whom being John Roberts. John owns a construction and maintenance company which was founded in 2006 after realising the demand for a contractor within the retail sector. Fast forward over more than a decade, and the company now employs more than 50 members of staff and has a clientele which includes mainstream brands such as Tesco, Nando's and Amazon.

The second entrepreneur I interviewed is Paul Thomas, who owns Synecore, a mechanical and electrical contractor with clients including Pret-A-Manger, Holiday Inn and KFC. Paul established Synecore 15 years ago, and has built the company into a 39 employee-strong business operating across the UK.

To add to the information collected from these two entrepreneurs, I have spent countless hours watching interviews and reading books and articles about various others, both from entrepreneurs of the present day, and entrepreneurs from centuries ago. This has enabled me able to identify patterns and themes between them, enabling me to pinpoint the characteristics and traits which have repeatedly led to success. I have also spent time researching Richard Branson and Mark Cuban, entrepreneurs who I look up to and consider role models. Without even realising, this book has become somewhat of a formula for success as an entrepreneur.

Before continuing, it is important to understand what is meant by the term 'entrepreneur', and what exactly a characteristic is.

The definition of an entrepreneur[i] is 'a person who sets up a business or businesses, taking on financial risks in the hope for profit.' The creation of any business involves some degree of investment, whether that be spending millions or simply buying a laptop. In my case, the 'financial risk' that I took involved spending £20 to buy a second-hand waffle making machine. As soon as you make an investment into something that can hopefully return a profit, you become an entrepreneur. Obviously, becoming an entrepreneur takes time and planning, yet interestingly, Richard Branson stated in his biography that with his first business venture of 'Student Magazine' which he started whilst still in school, 'without even knowing what the word meant, I was becoming an entrepreneur.'[ii] In his case, becoming an entrepreneur was just a matter of fate and circumstance, instead of being something which he planned and thought out.

In any business, the entrepreneur is usually the leader. Because the entrepreneur is the one who devised the business idea and put it into practise, the entrepreneur usually takes the role of the leader within the business. This position is commonly known as the 'CEO' which stands for 'Chief Executive Officer', however many entrepreneurs name the role differently. Anyone whom the entrepreneur employs after founding the business works for the entrepreneur, therefore putting him/her in the most prominent position within the company.

Paul Thomas made the point that being an entrepreneur and running a business is relatively simple and that anyone can do it. He outlined how there is "no great science to it", "no magic to it" and described it as "no different to running a household". He also outlined how a qualification is not needed for someone to become an entrepreneur, making entrepreneurship extremely accessible. Anyone can become an entrepreneur.

A characteristic is by definition;[iii] 'A feature or quality belonging typically to a person, place or thing and serving to identify them.' These 'features' can be physical, like hair colour, gender and height. However when looking at the characteristics which make a successful entrepreneur, it generally refers to the psychological ones. Everyone possesses a mixture of different characteristics which make up one's 'character'. Each person's combination of characteristics is what sets everyone apart from each other, if we were all to share the same characteristics then we would all look, think and behave in exactly the same way. If we all had the same characteristics, the world would be a very boring place!

When explaining what characteristics are, I like to compare it to a game of poker, imagining that each card represents a different characteristic. At the start of the game, each player is dealt their cards. Some of the cards are good cards, some not so useful. Some are dealt at the start, however more cards can be accrued as the game goes on. The number of good cards you acquire determines your potential to win the game, if you have several really good cards, you are more likely to achieve success than the players with the less desirable cards.

The same logic can be applied to entrepreneurship. There are certain characteristics a person can have, which we will consider later, that increase the chance of the person achieving success as an entrepreneur.

The definition of a characteristic also states how they are 'serving to identify them'. This suggests that someone's characteristics are at one's disposal, which they can choose to use if they so desire. In the poker example, if the poker player simply stares at the cards and never uses them, then despite being dealt a great hand, they will never win the game.

Innovation is the fundamental component of any entrepreneur. Entrepreneurs are people who understand a problem or demand and provide a solution, and because of that, all entrepreneurs require innovation to start a business. Usually, the more innovative an entrepreneurial idea is, the more likely it is to be successful. In fact, a biography written about Henry Ford explained how 'he credited his success to the inspiration behind his innovative mind.'[iv] Innovation could be classed as a characteristic of a successful entrepreneur, but in reality, innovation is a compulsory factor in becoming an entrepreneur. Innovation is what creates entrepreneurs, therefore every entrepreneur has some degree of innovation within them.

What does success mean to an entrepreneur?

I was talking to a friend of mine recently and asked him whether he considered me to be successful in business. He replied by telling me I was hugely successful, to which I was surprised. I thought that society's view of a successful entrepreneur involves big houses and nice cars, and I had neither! I may not be a millionaire from selling waffles for 3 years, but considering I started with a £20 second-hand machine in a farmer's market one winters morning means I have come a long way. The growth that the business has achieved in three years can therefore be considered successful.

In order to find out the characteristics which make successful entrepreneurs, it is imperative to understand what success means to entrepreneurs. This is key in enabling us to work out exactly what the characteristics which make the entrepreneurs successful are used to achieve.

The term success is greatly ambiguous as it cannot be defined by a single measurement or observation. Furthermore, success is perceived differently by different people, what one person considers success to be may be completely different from someone else.

The reason why people use the amount of money someone has or someone's 'financial worth' to measure their wealth is because it is easy to compare. The amount of money someone has is a quantitative value, meaning the amount of money that two people have can be easily compared. However, there are many factors of success which are less easily comparable, so are often overlooked. Many entrepreneurs start their own businesses for many different reasons, an example being the want for more control over how they spend their time.

The dictionary definition of success is 'the accomplishment of an aim or purpose'. As mentioned, entrepreneurs have different aims or purposes when starting out in business. If your aim is to simply make more time for yourself, then setting up a business which enables you to do so means that you have achieved success. Likewise, if the aim of the business is to make ten thousand pounds, one million pounds, or even one billion pounds, then the entrepreneur would be considered successful if that goal is realised.

As seen earlier, the definition of an entrepreneur is 'a person who sets up a business or businesses, taking up financial risks in the hope of profit'. In this definition, it clearly states that the aim and purpose of an entrepreneur is to make a profit. In theory, this suggests that an entrepreneur should be considered successful once a profit is made, but is this really the case?

Using John Roberts as an example, although setting up his business simply in the hope of amassing more monetary wealth, he only considered himself successful around 18 months after the creation of the company. He did not feel successful after first making a profit, it took a lot more than simply turning a profit for him to feel true success. In fact, there were many more factors than simply the amount of money made before he considered himself successful. He considered himself a success due to other factors such as "pleasure within the workplace", having financial freedom and having the flexibility to work wherever he wants, whenever he wants.

In a 'businessnewsdaily.com' survey, 16 entrepreneurs were asked for their definitions of success. The results were truly surprising.

I have produced a graph on the following page documenting their responses, with how many times various meanings of success were mentioned. Note that there are more than sixteen points as almost all of the entrepreneurs in question answered with multiple meanings of success.

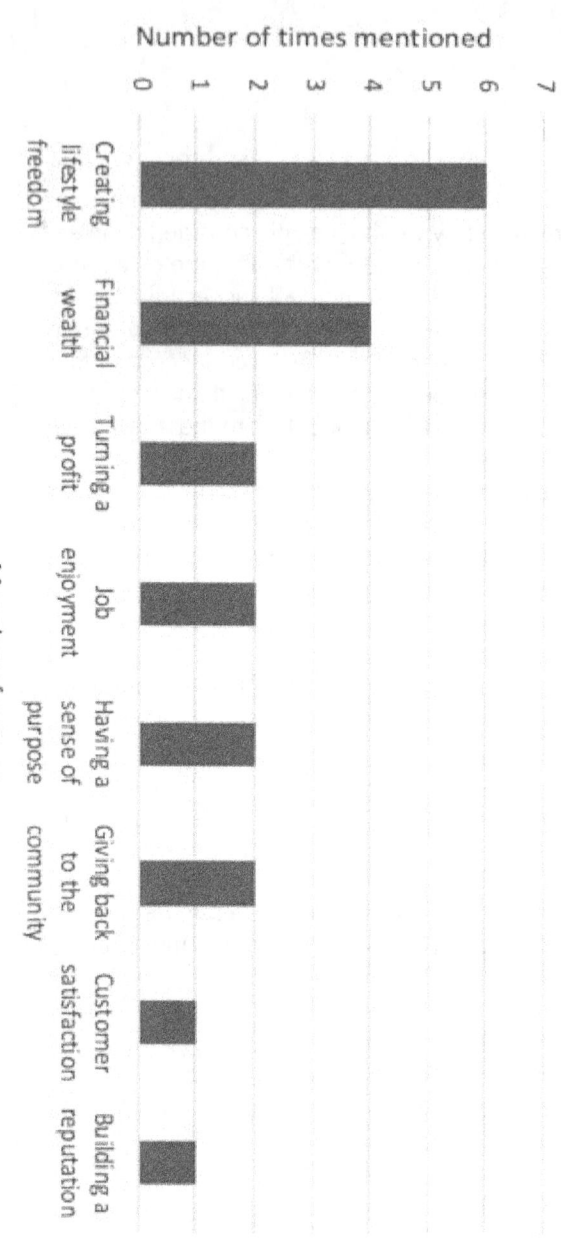

Creating a freedom of lifestyle granted through being your own boss was mentioned more times as a meaning of success than financial wealth! One of the entrepreneurs stated that "success to me is being able to spend your life in your own way", whilst another defined his success as "creating independence and freedom for myself through ideas and hard work". Creating a freedom of lifestyle that comes about by being your own boss became apparent as a central theme of the survey. Having the freedom to choose when and for how long to spend time working was worth much more to the entrepreneurs than the financial benefit of owning a successful business, yet this is something that cannot be measured objectively.

Now when looking at the question of should an entrepreneur be considered successful when first turning a profit, most of the entrepreneurs in the survey would disagree. They would say that there is much more to success than not just simply making a profit, but even making a lot of money. Richard Branson agrees, and wrote in his autobiography how "I'm not motivated by more money in my bank account", but instead believes that spending time with his family is much more valuable.

I think the idea that an entrepreneur can be considered successful after first making a profit is somewhat correct. However, the more money that the entrepreneur makes after that point can be used to measure the extent of the success.

Another interesting point is that when I asked the two entrepreneurs what success meant to them, they both mentioned similar ideas within their answers. Both Paul and John described how they felt success because they had created a business which makes money when they are not there. Through hard work over the years, they had been able to create the foundation from which their employees can operate in, which makes the business money. In other words, if they were to not to touch anything within the business ever again, it has been set up in a way that will continue to make money. A profit making formula.

Paul described it having a 'structure' in place that continues to produce a profit, whilst John described it as creating the "foundation and structure" of a business from which money can be made, which in turn grants him a constant and reliable income, even when he is absent.

Another similarity between the answers the two entrepreneurs gave was how success isn't a sudden occurrence. In John's case, he didn't wake up one morning and something suddenly happened which made him suddenly consider himself a success; instead he described it as being a "gradual change". Paul reflected this idea and stated how "it didn't happen overnight". This points to the idea that success in business takes time. For both entrepreneurs, putting the foundation in place for a reliable and predictable stream of profit took years. Becoming a successful entrepreneur is a gradual thing, which takes time, patience and consistent hard work.

A Guide to the Characteristics of the Successful Entrepreneur

Linking back to my experience of entrepreneurship, an important aspect to understand is the assumption that success as an entrepreneur is relative to the 'financial risk' taken when starting the business. Because I only invested £20 to fund the business, the return on the money invested is really high. However, when compared to a business which, for example, invests £3 million and makes £1 million profit, their return on investment is smaller. They have made more profit, but have not made as much money relative to the amount invested in the first place. Does this make me a more successful entrepreneur?

The final factor in understanding the success of an entrepreneur concerns philanthropism. During the course of my research into a range of successful entrepreneurs, I noticed a pattern amongst all of them which I could use as a measure of their success. I noticed that generally, the more successful the entrepreneur, the greater their involvement in philanthropy.

Philanthropism is defined as 'the desire to promote the welfare of others, expressed especially by the generous donation of money to good causes'[v], and for an entrepreneur it means in short, giving your money away. Many of the entrepreneurs I have researched believe it to be morally correct to donate money to those who do not live as comfortably as they do. The great industrialist JD Rockefeller was quoted as saying "I believe it is a duty for a man to get all the money he honestly can and give all he can", whilst Andrew Carnegie, a famous entrepreneur from the same era as Rockefeller, wrote in his biography how "the man who dies rich, dies disgraced."

Let's take some entrepreneurs with different levels of wealth and look at their contribution to philanthropy:

- Andrew Carnegie was a Scottish industrialist, who after ventures in the steel making and railroad industries, became one of the richest men in history with an estimated net worth of over $300 billion in today's money. Once he had finished his business career, it was claimed that he "dedicated 100% of himself through philanthropy" to the point that "giving his money away became his occupation".

- Bill Gates, with a net worth of over $100 billion, is planning to give all of his wealth away. He has so far successfully donated over $45 billion through the Bill and Melinda Gates foundation.

- Mark Cuban is another American entrepreneur who has found success in the technology industry and has since become a TV personality. He has an estimated net worth of $4.3 billion. His work in philanthropy has involved a $10 million donation to 'promote women in leadership roles and combat domestics violence', as well as spending time to help disadvantaged entrepreneurs who have less opportunity.

- In John Roberts' case, his contribution to philanthropy has included acts such as sponsoring local football teams, and he once gave a homeless man £50 out of pure generosity outside a fast-food restaurant.

Do you see the pattern here? Generally speaking, the more successful the entrepreneur is, the greater their involvement in philanthropy, and the greater the proportion of their wealth is donated.

Key takeaways from this section:

- Success as an entrepreneur isn't necessarily defined by the amount of money made, but if the goal when becoming an entrepreneur has been realised.
- The meaning of success for most entrepreneurs is enjoying the freedom that being your own boss grants you with.
- True business success is having instilled a structure in place to make money without the entrepreneur having to work.
- The extent of an entrepreneur's philanthropy can be used as a measure of their success.

How do entrepreneurs gain the characteristics which lead them to success?

Nature vs nurture. It is one of the largest ongoing debates, and finding the answer would completely change the way we understand human behaviour. Are the characteristics which a successful entrepreneur possesses genetically gifted to them by their parents, or are they learnt through interaction with other people and their environment? In this chapter, we are looking at how successful entrepreneurs believe they acquired the characteristics which have led them to success, and whether the science agrees with them.

Understanding how entrepreneurs gain certain characteristics is key if you are striving to become a successful entrepreneur. Understanding the following information will enable you to know if and how you are able to gain the necessary characteristics. For example, if we conclude that certain characteristics key to the success of entrepreneurs are 100% inherited at birth, then you as an entrepreneur will understand that these characteristics, if not possessed already, will be impossible to acquire. Likewise, if the characteristic of leadership, for example, is gained by spending time around great leaders, then you will realise that you have the ability to acquire leadership as a characteristic yourself.

Throughout my research, I have come across many entrepreneurs explaining how their personality and certain characteristics they possess have been passed to them through their genes. In Richard Branson's autobiography, he describes himself as a "born optimist". Optimism, one of the main characteristics responsible for him taking the 'Virgin' brand into so many industries and becoming so successful, he believes was with him from birth. He also describes how he has a "competitive instinct", another characteristic he is convinced is key to his success, and another that he believes was inherited. The book frequently hinted towards the notion that his characteristics which have been most influential to his success were with him since birth.

Furthermore, out of the range of entrepreneurs I researched, almost all of them had shown signs of entrepreneurship from a young age. Showing glimpses of entrepreneurship during childhood is a trait which many successful entrepreneurs share. The American billionaire Mark Cuban showed signs of entrepreneurship during his youth through small businesses he set up, his first one selling baseball cards when he was only 12 years old. In an interview with Yahoo Finance[vi], he explained how he knew from a young age of his 'hustler' mentality, which he believed was inherited from his father, the son of a Russian immigrant who worked 6 days a week. This shows how the 'hustler' characteristic most probably runs in the family. When asked whether entrepreneurs are born or built, he explained how he feels he has always been 'wired' towards entrepreneurship. The term 'wired' suggests he feels as if he was born with entrepreneurship already integrated into his character, almost as if he was destined to become an entrepreneur. Similarly, Richard Branson explained how "at heart I am an entrepreneur", reflecting Cuban's suggestion of a natural ability for entrepreneurship.

When Henry Ford was thirteen, his grandfather gave him his pocket watch, to which he "promptly took apart and reassembled". This indicated that from such a young age, he had a natural ability for mechanics and the understanding of how things worked. Evidently, this passion which was apparent at only thirteen years old was later responsible for the creation of the first mass produced automobile, which went on to change the way the world travelled. He was in possession of the characteristic which was so influential to his success, during his childhood. As previously mentioned, he was described as crediting his success to "the inspiration behind his innovative mind", again suggesting that he was naturally gifted with the characteristic which generated him so much success in his adult life.

Furthermore, John Roberts provides another example of an entrepreneur showing characteristics at a young age which would later influence his success. He credits self-confidence as one of the key characteristics behind his success, which he argues he has had since a child. One day when still at school, his teacher remarked to him how "you will argue in black and white". He believes this self-confidence, which was evident in his childhood, is the same characteristic which has played such an important role in his success as an entrepreneur.

Many successful entrepreneurs have shown signs of entrepreneurship, or characteristics which will later help them in business, from a young age. Because they have these traits and characteristics with such little experience, it has to suggest that they have been inherited. Interestingly however, Paul Thomas is an exception to the rule, who showed no signs of entrepreneurship during his youth, describing himself as a 'typical teenager'.

The final point in support of the 'nature' argument is due to the research conducted around personality inheritance. Gordon Allport, an American psychologist who is often referred to as one of the founding figures of 'personality psychology', theorised the trait theory[vii]. The theory states that one's personality is comprised completely of traits inherited from their parents. This means that behaviour is 'innate and genetically programmed'. Every characteristic and all behaviour of an individual is a result of their genetics which are determined from birth. Therefore, in Allport's opinion, the characteristics which make entrepreneurs successful are likewise inherited from birth. If you are not gifted with certain characteristics when you are born, the chances of becoming a successful entrepreneur are much slimmer.

The German Psychologist Hans Eysenck reflected the idea of inheritance through his work. In 1947, he conducted a survey of over fifty people[viii], using a 'personality-measuring' machine. With the information collected, Eysenck could categorise the participants into either having extroverted or introverted personalities. He believed that the personality type that people have is determined at birth, in correlation with Allport's trait theory. It would therefore imply that successful entrepreneurs are fortunate in being gifted a personality which would greatly increase their chance of becoming a success in business.

Now let's look at the other side of the argument, which is the idea that the characteristics common among successful entrepreneurs have been acquired *since* birth. Unlike the theory that all characteristics are determined genetically, this is the belief that the characteristics have been learnt through experience and interaction with the environment. This way, the entrepreneurs have been able to select, or almost 'hand-pick' certain characteristics to add to their personalities, in order to maximise their chance of success. If this theory is correct, then it would mean that anyone can acquire the characteristics of a successful entrepreneur!

Despite the likes of Mark Cuban and Richard Branson expressing the opinion that they believe certain characteristics which have helped them to success have been with them forever, there are also many examples of entrepreneurs of the opposite opinion. Henry Ford was described as having "acquired the trait of being persistent and carried it without recognition."[ix] The term 'acquired' clearly shows how he has learnt the characteristic of perseverance, added it to his character and used it to his advantage.

Likewise, Paul Thomas doesn't agree with the idea that the characteristics of a successful entrepreneur are predetermined. Instead, the characteristics which he attributes to his success, he believes were learnt throughout his life. He believes that tenacity, a characteristic which he credits as being most important to his success, was learnt through his experience working as a salesman. The process of repeatedly knocking on the same doors until securing a deal, instilled a tenaciousness into him which he then carried forward into his business career. He therefore believes he was not born with tenacity already engraved into his personality, but acquired it through experience.

JP Morgan, arguably the most powerful banker and financier in American history was described in a profile of his as the following; "If Morgan didn't have these traits that were instilled by his father and learned in business, he wouldn't be able to create the success and influence around what he did."[x] This description clearly explains how the characteristics which were key to his success were learnt from the environment. The term 'instilled' suggests that his father gradually established these traits into him from a young age. The description also points out that without the characteristics which were *learnt* in business, then he simply wouldn't have reached the level of success and influence he subsequently achieved.

When speaking to John and Paul, they both agreed that they have acquired the characteristic of leadership and the skill of managing people since starting in business. A characteristic fundamental in running a successful business with numerous staff didn't come naturally to them, and that they acquired the characteristic after years of running their businesses. This shows that leadership, a characteristic so important in the success of both of their businesses, was learnt *since* they became entrepreneurs, and that they didn't have the characteristic from birth.

Another argument in favour of characteristics being acquired through experience is to do with who you spend most of your time around. The theory is known as the 'proximity effect', and suggests that your behaviour and habits are most influenced by the people with whom you spend the most time interacting with. In an episode of the American TV series 'Shark Tank', one of the contestants said to the camera after leaving the interview room; "hang around with four broke people and you'll be the fifth".

If you were to spend more time around drug takers, then drug taking will start to seem normal, so you are more inclined to take drugs. Likewise, if you start spending most of your time around charitable people, you will feel naturally inclined to involve yourself more in charity. This same reasoning applies for acquiring characteristics which build personality. If you spend more time around hateful or obnoxious people, there is a greater chance that these characteristics will be absorbed into your own personality. This can therefore become a powerful tool for entrepreneurs. By spending time around successful entrepreneurs, you will be able to gradually acquire certain characteristics from them, sometimes without even realising.

The 'proximity effect' can also be used as a counterargument against some of the Mark Cuban and Henry Ford examples mentioned previously. One of the reasons why Cuban believes he has the characteristic of being a 'hustler' is because he inherited it through his father, as he displayed the same characteristic as his Dad. However, the proximity effect could suggest that he acquired the characteristic because he spent the majority of his childhood with his father. As a child, the people you interact with and spend most of your time around is your parents, so did Cuban really receive the 'hustler' trait genetically, or was it because the majority of his social interaction when he was younger was with his dad, and therefore he gained the 'hustler' characteristic through his environment? Since the person who he spent the most time around was his father, he was exposed to the 'hustler' characteristic, which may have resulted in him naturally thinking and behaving in the same way.

The concept of the 'proximity effect' links nicely to Bandura's social learning theory.[xi] Bandura postulated the theory after his experiment with the 'Bobo Doll'. The 'Bobo Doll'[xii] experiment conducted in the 1960's involved two groups of children. The first group were shown a video of someone behaving aggressively towards the doll. The second group were shown a video of someone acting less aggressively towards the doll. When subsequently put into the room with the doll, the children who watched the aggressive video acted aggressively towards the doll, both physically and verbally. On the other hand, the group who were shown the non-aggressive video acted in a much calmer way when presented with the doll, playing with it more as a toy rather than a punching bag.

From the results of the experiment, Bandura concluded that humans acquire characteristics such as aggression through the process of 'observational learning', which means watching the behaviour of another person. Banduras 'social learning' theory would therefore suggest that the characteristics which a successful entrepreneur possesses are obtainable through observing behaviour. Bandura would argue that Cuban picked up the 'hustler' characteristic by observing his father. Likewise, observing the ways of successful entrepreneurs and watching their behaviour will result in you naturally acquiring their characteristics.

At the end of the day, it is up to you as a reader to decide which side of the argument you take, whether you believe that the characteristics of a successful entrepreneur can be learnt, or are simply programmed from birth. However, there is another viewpoint to add, and in my opinion the most logical. This is the idea that some characteristics of a successful entrepreneur are genetically determined from birth, however some can be acquired through experience, almost a combination between the two arguments.

One way to describe this idea is by using the poker example from the very start of the book which was the idea that your characteristics can be compared to the cards you are given at the start of the game. Imagine the cards given to you as representing your portfolio of characteristics; some are good, some not so good. However, the cards given are only useful when used in the game. If they are not used, they will simply sit on the table as worthless pieces of coloured card with numbers on. The same applies with your characteristics. If you know you have the gift of certain characteristics, it is up to you to apply them within everyday life effectively in order to yield the benefit with which they provide you. Otherwise, these genetically gifted characteristics will not be used to their full potential.

When speaking to John Roberts, he presented his belief that the characteristics which he attributes to his success have always been with him, but it was up to him to figure out what they were, and then to use them effectively. He believes that some characteristics are genetically determined; you are born with them. However, these characteristics are "unlocked" when put into a certain situation or environment. People inherit their core characteristics and abilities at birth which are then "unlocked" at certain points in life when needed most, or when circumstance forces them to be used. If the son of a world champion body builder has been given the natural ability to acquire muscle easily, his muscles will never increase in size until he goes to the gym. By going to the gym and lifting weights, the bodybuilder gene is 'unlocked'. In John's case, he believes he was born with a natural ability for entrepreneurship, but it was his effort and determination which enabled that ability to surface.

This idea of a combination of genetically inherited characteristics and those which can be learnt through the environment is reflected in the work of the psychologist Hollander. Hollander presented the 'interactionist perspective'[xiii], which attempts to explain how personality is formed through both genetic and environmental influences. The idea is that the traits we are born with can be altered to best suit the situation. For example, an entrepreneur who is naturally aggressive and ruthless may act in a less assertive manner, and much calmer when talking to young apprentices within the company, because the situation requires a different approach to the way that the genetics may formulate.

Hollander proposed that personality is comprised of three main areas; the psychological core, the typical responses and the role-related behaviour.

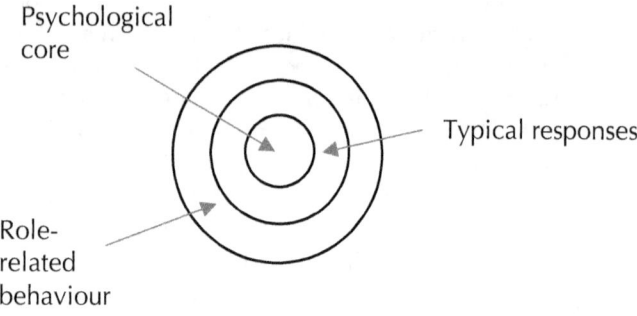

The psychological core represents the inherited traits and core beliefs of the individual. These are underlying and highly unlikely to change. This is the section of your personality which is comprised of genetic information and in John's case, includes the fundamental characteristics of his success. The typical responses are the usual reaction someone would make to a given situation, which is predictable due to the fact that they are heavily influenced by the psychological core, which doesn't change. The role related behaviour is the furthest away from the core, so is the most likely to be affected by the environment. In the case of entrepreneurs, this is where characteristics can be gained or adapted to meet the needs of the situation.

Hollander's interactionist theory agrees with the understanding that an entrepreneur is born with the fundamental, or 'core' characteristics which are inherited. However, experience and the environment can affect how these characteristics are applied, and results in new appropriate characteristics being added to one's personality.

Both Hollander's and John's approaches point to the idea that the characteristics of a successful entrepreneur are gained through a *combination* of inherited genetics and environmental factors. In my opinion, this approach is the most accurate of the three as I believe characteristics are inherited, yet the environment must have an influence on one's personality. For me, the idea that experiences and circumstances have no effect on the characteristics which someone possesses is completely irrational, you surely cannot end life with the exact same characteristics as when you were born. In my four-year experience as an entrepreneur, my personality has undoubtedly changed, and I have most definitely picked up characteristics and skills from successful entrepreneurs with whom I have spent time with.

As an entrepreneur, it is imperative to identify which are your core characteristics, and which ones you require to increase the chance of becoming a successful entrepreneur. The three most important characteristics will be explained later in this guide.

Key takeaways from this section;

- Many successful entrepreneurs showed signs of entrepreneurship from a young age, however it is not essential.
- Some of the characteristics of successful entrepreneurs are inherited, some learnt through experience.
- By spending time around successful entrepreneurs, you will naturally acquire their characteristics.
- You should decide which are the characteristics of a successful entrepreneur you are lacking.

Louis Callaghan-Inge

How have the characteristics of a successful entrepreneur changed over time?

In such a technologically advanced world, dominated by huge multinational corporations, the characteristics of a successful entrepreneur have had to adapt to the changing times. The characteristics of a successful entrepreneur today are undoubtedly different from those of previously successful entrepreneurs, who achieved their success decades or centuries ago. So, to what extent are the characteristics of the successful entrepreneur today different from those of previous generations? Besides, are there some characteristics which have remained fundamental to entrepreneurial success throughout every age of entrepreneurship, are there certain keys to success which are common regardless of the industry and the period in history?

As an entrepreneur reading this in the 21st century, understanding the characteristics of currently successful entrepreneurs will be key in achieving your success. We live in a world so distant from the one in which the great historical entrepreneurs have thrived in, hence some of their keys to success may not be applicable to an entrepreneur of today. For example, by simply employing every characteristic of a famous 19th century entrepreneur to your character today, they may not be relevant or useful to the present age, and therefore reaching entrepreneurial success may become stunted. Understanding the characteristics common among successful entrepreneurs of this generation will help fast-track your success.

This section will focus on the story of entrepreneurship and explain how the characteristics which have help entrepreneurs achieve success have changed over time.

The story of entrepreneurship has its origins as far back as 20,000 years ago, to a time where a vast proportion of the planet was still covered in ice. In what is current day Papua New Guinea, evidence of the earliest known entrepreneurship was recorded, where local tribes would trade obsidian, a type of volcanic glass used in hunting in exchange for other valuables such as food and building materials. This early form of entrepreneurship continued for millennia, involving trade between tribes and groups in order to provide extra supplies or comfort.

But it was at the start of the agricultural revolution where entrepreneurship evolved into the force that would change the world forever. The agricultural revolution was when hunter-gatherer tribes came to the realisation that it would make more sense to domesticate plants and animals for food, instead of continually hunting for their food. This led to the creation of the first towns and villages, as people now had a fixed, reliable food source. With the excess produce that a farmer would grow and not eat, they could bargain with villagers to give them something that they considered equally valuable, maybe a different type of food, as a trade for his time growing the crop. Due to the formation of towns and villages, it enabled some of the population to specialise in crafts such as the making of clothes or pottery for example. These were the first entrepreneurs, selling their products and services for profit! Arguably, these entrepreneurs were the most innovative, as they were not just the first to sell goods for a profit, but they invented entrepreneurship entirely!

As towns and villages grew in size and standards of living increased, entrepreneurs continuously saw opportunities for profit when a problem arose, meaning their innovation shaped the way society was formed and how it operated.

The next important event in the story of entrepreneurship happened when the first recorded trading occurred between cultures. Around 2000 BC, the first cities were formed, and shortly after, different civilisations and empires were making contact with one another. Unsurprisingly, the most innovative realised that profits could be made by exchanging goods and ideas between cities and cultures. Trade routes were quickly established, meaning exotic fruits could be exchanged between Africa and Europe, or gunpowder from China to the rest of the world, for example.

Prior to the invention of money, entrepreneurs would barter goods for other goods, in the hope that the commodity they were receiving would be more valuable than those they supplied. This meant that the skill of selling was key, and was the most important factor in being a successful entrepreneur at the time. Having the persuasion and skill to sell something was the critical difference between a successful entrepreneur and an unsuccessful one, and was the difference between putting food on the table for your family or having them go hungry. However, the creation of money acted as a more accurate measure of the value of a product, and gave entrepreneurs the ability to put prices on certain goods. The earliest forms of currency included things like seashells, rocks and rare metals such as silver. Money and coins as we know of today were only invented around 600BC, and the first can be traced to what is now modern-day Turkey, involving a metal disk with an imprint of a lion.

Yet it was not always plain sailing for entrepreneurs. During the middle ages, as the Christian church was gaining power and in control of most of Europe and the Middle East, the idea of self-gained wealth was shunned upon by society. People were forced to pay 10% of their wages to the church known as a 'tithe', which many people believed should have been more for those businesspeople who were considered 'well-off'. There was also the notion that the greater donation of one's wealth given to the church, the greater the likelihood of reaching heaven, so many entrepreneurs felt obliged to donate larger sums of money. To add to this, the belief that God had created the world perfectly meant that entrepreneurial innovation was deemed to be altering God's faultless world, so innovation became stifled. In some cases, innovation was even punishable by death!

At this stage in the story of entrepreneurship, these entrepreneurs were known more as explorers than entrepreneurs. When European explorers reached new lands, such as Columbus' discovery of America in the late 15th century, they realised that the newly discovered land brought with it a vast new range of materials and goods, which provided them with the potential for huge profits if brought back home. This realisation made the early explorers some of the richest people in history relative to their time, and many argue this period established the beginnings of capitalism as we know it today.

One of the main characteristics which made successful explorer/entrepreneurs was that they were huge risk takers. Sailing in a direction never taken before, to hopefully find undiscovered lands with finite supplies of food and water was a huge risk, they didn't know if they would even find anything at all, or whether they would return to port safely. Not to mention the goods that they brought back, filling the boat with goods that didn't satisfy the European taste of the time would possibly mean no profit would be made, so a trip which could potentially take years may have been made in vain.

The explorers of that time also had to have an abundance of perseverance and resilience. Going for months without touching land must have been unimaginably demoralising, so having the resilience to not give up and turn around required strong characters.

The industrial revolution was the next major event in the history of entrepreneurship. The reason for entrepreneurship having such a boost during this time was mainly due to two factors: Firstly, new inventions such as coal and steam power meant goods could be produced much quicker and more efficiently, swiftly abolishing the need for weather dependant wind-powered sources of energy. Secondly, large-scale urbanisation involving people flocking to cities in their millions, meaning that there was a huge demand for low-paid employment. Companies saw this as great opportunity, as it meant labour costs, commonly the most expensive outgoing for any business, could be kept to a minimum. These two factors allowed for goods to be produced on a much larger scale, meaning more profit could be made.

This period turned some entrepreneurs into not just some of the most famous entrepreneurs in history, but some of the most famous *people* in history, and into individuals whose legacy's still shape the way we live today. The likes of Henry Ford, J.D Rockefeller and JP Morgan are still household names, even more than a century after their deaths.

Henry Ford is arguably the most prominent entrepreneur of all time. Henry was born into a humble Michigan farming family the 1860's, and showed signs of being an avid mechanic and engineer from a very young age. After experimenting with and developing the gas engine and gas-powered vehicles, he founded the 'Ford Motor Company' in 1903. The genius of the company was not only the cars themselves, but the process by which they were made. He was the first person to utilise the 'assembly line' production process, whereby the construction of his cars involved different parts being added together in sequence, until the final product was eventually assembled. This technique of mass production was revolutionary, and is the basis of almost all modern day production of goods.

The story of Henry Ford points to the characteristic of persistence as key to his success. In an article written about Henry[xiv], it stated that he was "persistent to the core" and that "before being successful, Henry had initiated two other companies pertaining to the sole purpose of developing automobile machinery. Although, he introduced the companies, they were soon shut down." His story of unforgiving trial and error until eventually achieving success outlines how persistence was maybe the single characteristic of his most responsible for his success. In Henry's book 'My Life and Work'[xv], he states that "Failure is only the opportunity more intelligently to begin again."

Another industrialist of the period who left his mark on history was Andrew Carnegie. Like Henry Ford and many other successful entrepreneurs, Carnegie came from humble beginnings. Born in Scotland in 1835 into "abject poverty"[xvi], his family moved to America when he was 13 years old in search of a better life. During the American civil war in the 1860's, he noticed that the wooden bridges were easily burnt or broken by the troops, so satisfied the demand for more reliable, iron-built bridges by creating the 'Keystone Bridge Company'. His next venture was to construct steel mills which would supply railroad companies. He sold this company when he was 70 years old, making him the wealthiest person in the world at the time. After selling the company, he focused 100% of his time to philanthropy, giving his vast wealth away to many good causes.

Like many entrepreneurs throughout history, it was Carnegie's work ethic that proved to be the characteristic key to his success. Even from his childhood, his intense and unrelenting work ethic was evident. Shortly after arriving in America he had to drop out of school to work, shovelling coal in boiler rooms in order to support his family. In his book written before his death, he wrote how "you cannot push anyone up the ladder unless he is willing to climb." This shows how important he believes it is to have a strong work ethic, without it you will never be able to reach success.

Another characteristic key to Carnegie's success, which is one he possessed more than many other successful entrepreneurs since, was his ruthlessness. An example being how, in an attempt to squeeze out as much profit as he could from the steel making business, he decided to cut the pay for his workers at his Homestead plant, whilst increasing their workload. Unsurprisingly the workers went on strike, so Carnegie decided to simply substitute his workers for lower skilled immigrant workers who were willing to work for less pay. Whilst the new workers were entering the factory, a fight broke out between the two groups, in which 16 people died and hundreds more were injured, in a day which would later become known as the 'Homestead Massacre'.

Another example of Carnegie's ruthlessness involved the story of 'Duquene works', a competitor to Carnegie's steel mills. In an attempt to put them out of business, Carnegie spread a false rumour about how the steel being made from the Duquene mills was faulty, and that railroad companies doing business with them would be getting a poor-quality product. The plan worked, and it put Duquene's finances in ruins, so much so that Carnegie bought them out himself for a bargain price! Nothing was actually wrong with the steel from the plant, yet Carnegie's ruthlessness had enabled him to expand his steel-producing monopoly and greatly increase his control over the industry.

This ruthlessness that Carnegie had within his character brought him enormous success. It provided him with greater profit margins, more control over his employees, and dirty business tricks gave him less competition.

It could be argued that success for entrepreneurs in the industrial era required them to be a good deal bolder, take bigger risks and be more ruthless than current day entrepreneurs. This is because the presence of workers unions were much stronger, meaning the entrepreneurs had to be more controlling in order to keep their workers in line. Furthermore, the unfair control that these entrepreneurs had over their employees allowed them to become as ruthless as they desired, as there was very little the workers could do to fight back. The idea of the wealthy industrialists being ruthless and taking advantage of their workers for their own benefit became such a shared belief throughout society that the term 'robber baron' was coined. The 'robber baron' became the stereotype for the cold-blooded, rich businessmen of the time, who "would stop at nothing to achieve great wealth"[xvii].

It is also important to mention this is the period in the story of entrepreneurship where the first female entrepreneurs came to significance. Up to this point in history, unless born into royalty or a high-status family, women were seen as secondary to men. The same belief was shared between almost every culture in the world, where the men of the house were the 'breadwinners', who would spend their days working in order to provide their families with food to eat and clothes to wear. Women on the other hand were expected to stay at home to look after the children, cook, clean and tend to the man of the house. Because of society's expectations of women at the time, entrepreneurship for a woman was therefore never an option.

In today's society, female entrepreneurs are accepted as equally as men, yet this was not always the case. As mentioned above, the expectation of women was to stay at home to tender to the family's needs, and therefore becoming an entrepreneur as a woman was unheard of. The first women to break the mould and to be noticed as the first successful female entrepreneur was Madam C J Walker. Walker, like many descendance of the slave trade, was born on a cotton plantation in the south of the United States in 1867. Because of the poor hygiene conditions the slaves were forced to live under, many women experienced chronic hair loss. This was until her concoction of Vaseline and sulphur claimed to cure the problem, which she started selling to women in her community. As the business grew, she opened a factory employing only women, and was successful enough to help lift fellow African American slaves out of poverty. She is now considered the 'mother of female entrepreneurship' after her breakthrough and inspirational story, and single handily re-wrote the impression of women in society.

Shortly after Madam Walker's success, many more influential female entrepreneurs would make their own mark on history such as Coco Chanel, who's revolutionary designs have changed the way women have dressed ever since. The characteristic most important to her success was her imagination, by designing clothes and accessories which scrapped the old fashioned long flowing dresses with shorter and slimmer ones.

Since the era of Madam C J Walker and Coco Chanel who were the pioneers of female entrepreneurship, further significant events such as the suffragette movement which gave women the right to vote, continued to elevate society's view of women to that equal of men, meaning female entrepreneurship is much more acceptable and accessible to women nowadays.

It was just after World War Two where the idea of a 'global economy' was understood. Advances in transport provided entrepreneurs with the ability to sell to customers all over the planet. This fuelled the takeover of multinational corporations such as banks and fast food chains, as they could now establish their brands in many more countries to maximise profits.

Despite all the events which have shaped the history of entrepreneurship into the powerful force it is today, arguably the most influential has only recently taken place; the rise of the internet.

The growth and influence of the internet has happened at an overwhelmingly fast pace. The 'World Wide Web' was only created in the 1980's, so to think of how much of our daily life is influenced by something so young is astonishing. As Richard Branson explains; "The internet has changed the way we consume information". In just over 30 years, the internet has taken over our lives, and is now the dominant means of communication, shopping and entertainment. The rise of the internet has changed the way we live like nothing before.

The internet has therefore had a huge impact on entrepreneurship, one arguably as influential as the agricultural and industrial revolutions. It means there has been a huge shift in so many aspects of our lives, for example how we purchase products, the products that companies sell, how companies advertise and employ, the list of changes that the internet has made to business is endless.

One big reason for the impact this technological revolution has made to entrepreneurship is due to convenience. People can now shop from anywhere and at any time of day. Instead of spending valuable time making a trip to a high street or marketplace look for things, a quick web search will take you to the product in seconds. By providing a vast range of websites and platforms to purchase the same product, consumers can easily compare goods to find the cheapest options. If I wanted to order something online, a new book for example, I can type it into a search engine, purchase it within seconds, and it will be with me in a matter of days, sometimes even the same day! No queueing at a checkout, no need to hunt around a shop for a certain book, no need to interact with anyone, and all for a cheaper price!

In fact, in a recent report commissioned by the law firm 'Womble Bond Dickenson'[xviii], online shopping will account for over 50% of total retail sales in the next ten years. And just like at any point in the story of entrepreneurship, change means the opportunity of profit for entrepreneurs. Entrepreneurs have capitalised on this societal change, with the creation of 'e-commerce' stores to supply this new demand. Many entrepreneurs have seen how convenience is such a factor of sales, therefore implementing things like shorter delivery times and reduced fees for delivery. Just like at any other time in the history of entrepreneurship, the 'internet entrepreneur' is meeting the needs of current demands, and capitalising.

The impact that the internet has made on entrepreneurship has had its effect on every business without exception, both positively and negatively. Paul and John, who both operate 'brick and mortar' businesses, have still been affected by the rise of the internet. Paul explained how the internet and social media allow for 24/7 advertising, and finding new clients and staff has been made so much more available. A useful improvement that both John and Paul agree on is that the internet has made communication considerably easier. Things such as emails and messaging on social media mean that communication between both employees and clients, such a crucial factor in running any business, is now much quicker and more straightforward.

perfect set of characteristics, no set formula for success, all entrepreneurs function differently.

Entrepreneurs will continue to shape history. It is the innovation of entrepreneurs from all corners of the world which has directed civilisation into what it is today, and it is entrepreneurship which will continue to determine how we live our lives. Without entrepreneurs, humanity may well still be stuck in the age of tribes and hunter gatherers. As Richard Branson put it; "It is entrepreneurs who have the potential to change the world."

you are competing with the whole world. Online shopping enables the consumer to compare the same product between hundreds of sites worldwide. Because of the high levels of competition, internet entrepreneurs have to make their websites or products stand out even more to potential customers, using online advertising space and aggressive marketing tactics.

Throughout history, the characteristics which have made entrepreneurs successful have differed depending on the time. Yet, there seems to be underlying commonalities which have been fundamental to entrepreneurial success, no matter the point in history. Whether it be selling tools to a fellow tribe to make weapons or selling cryptocurrency online, the same basic principles apply. As Branson writes about a career in business of over 50 years, "While business may have changed from when I started out, the principles are the same".

Yet, many successful entrepreneurs have different characteristics which have led them to success, the characteristics which may have helped one entrepreneur achieve success may not be the same as another. Carnegie reached success through ruthlessness with a 'win at all costs' attitude, whereas other entrepreneurs like Bill Gates for example, has reached the same level of success without being ruthless. Although some characteristics are required for success, there is no

Key takeaways from this section;

- Entrepreneurial success can be achieved through different methods; characteristics which work for some people may not work for others.
- The fundamental characteristics which lead to entrepreneurial success have been more or less the same throughout history and apply to every business.
- The internet is going to, and is fundamentally changing entrepreneurship and the way that business is done. Every form of entrepreneurship from now on will be somehow affected by the internet.

Louis Callaghan-Inge

Which are the three most important characteristics of the successful entrepreneur?

Now that we have completely understood everything surrounding the characteristics which make entrepreneurs successful, it is now time to look at the characteristics themselves in more detail. I could simply list a bunch of characteristics which different entrepreneurs consider to having helped them reach success, however this section is going to narrow down the 3 characteristics which have been the most influential in reaching success between the range of entrepreneurs that I have researched. During my research, these three characteristics have clearly stood out as being the characteristics not only the most frequently mentioned, but the characteristics which the entrepreneurs themselves have expressed the importance of.

As an entrepreneur reading this guidebook, implementing these three characteristics into your character today, or focusing on utilising their full potential if already acquired, will hopefully enable you to reach success quicker. Surely, the fastest and easiest way to reach success as an entrepreneur would be by following the ways of already successful entrepreneurs? The following characteristics are listed in order of importance.

Resilience

The characteristic of resilience is the most important characteristic in order to reach entrepreneurial success. Resilience is defined as 'the capacity to recover quickly from difficulties; toughness'. Every entrepreneur without fail will encounter difficulties during their business ventures, some more difficult than others. However it is the ability to recover, improve and learn from those difficulties which has proven so important in the success of so many entrepreneurs. Almost every entrepreneur I have researched has encountered some degree of failure before they reach success, and it is usually how they respond to that failure which determines whether they reach success or not. Resilience is by far the most common characteristic between successful entrepreneurs.

The term 'resilience' is really an umbrella term which incorporates the characteristics of a strong work ethic, determination and persistence, all of which have to be present in order to acquire the characteristic of resilience. Without these other factors, one's resilience would be much weaker, so they will not be able to recover from difficulty or failure as easily.

There are countless examples of resilience playing a key role in the success of entrepreneurs. Henry

Ford's story involved major failure before reaching success. In his first venture, 'The Detroit Automobile Company', the shareholders became 'sick' of Henry's lack of progress, and voted to kick him out. Despite this demoralising and embarrassing failure, he persisted, determined to make his dream of creating a vehicle cheap enough for the average man become a reality. Instead of giving up, he started another company, and we all know the story from there on. His story of significant failure before reaching success proves how the characteristic of perseverance was hugely influential. If he did not have strong perseverance, he could have easily given up on his dream, and the automobile industry may have never become what it is today.

Madam C J Walker was one of the first female entrepreneurs in America, at a time when discrimination against black people was the everyday norm, and when society's view of women was that they were weaker and less significant than men. To reach success from her lowly background was unbelievable. She had no role model or anyone to look up to; no woman had gone before her. The resilience of Madam C J Walker to not only become an entrepreneur, but thrive as one given her circumstance was monumental.

In a 2013 study[xxi] by the scientists Carayannis and Stewart from the Washington University School of Business, concluded that the most accurate way to describe a successful entrepreneur was as an 'obsessed maniac'. The term 'obsessed maniac' points to the idea that in order to reach success, an entrepreneur must become obsessed with the goal that is trying to be reached. Furthermore, 'maniac' implies that the distinguished entrepreneur must have an almost crazy and extremely enthusiastic work rate. This undoubtedly means that successful entrepreneurs must have an abundance of resilience in order to be continuously focused on achieving a vision. The study describes how common behaviour among the entrepreneurs they researched showed an "unrelenting persistence to pursue a vision".

Mark Cuban believes his 'hustler' mentality, his work ethic and resilience that were 'wired' in him from a young age have been instrumental in achieving his entrepreneurial success. In a recent interview with Yahoo Finance, he said, "I describe myself as a grinder" and that "If you're gonna be great at something, you gotta make the effort". These different points he makes all point to the same thing – that success doesn't come without resilience and hard work.

When speaking with Paul Thomas, he emphasised how he believes it was his 'tenacity' which was the characteristic most important to his success. Tenacity is defined as 'the quality or fact of continuing to exist; persistence', very similar to resilience. When attempting to attain the café chain 'Pret-A-Manger' as a client, he asked one of the managers over and over again for a meeting, sending email after email, before finally arranging a meeting and subsequently securing them as a client. This tenacity and resilience have been the characteristics most influential to his success, and without the level of resilience that Paul has, the company would never have been where it is today. As John Roberts believes, some people are born with natural levels of intelligence or knowledge, but without hard work and resilience it will never amount to anything.

I'm sure every successful entrepreneur in the history of business has their own stories and examples of how they have had to be resilient. Whether you label it as resilience, persistence, determination or tenacity, the idea that having the ability to carry on when things are not going as planned, and continuing until the goal is realised, is the fundamental characteristic most important to achieving success as an entrepreneur.

The desire to continuously learn and improve.

During the span of my research, I began to notice a pattern between almost all of the most successful entrepreneurs, one that I hadn't realised the importance of previously. A characteristic shared between them which is so obviously logical, yet one that I had never been aware of before. The common theme between the entrepreneurs that I researched, is that all of them have an unbelievable desire to learn, whether that be about their products, their industry, their competitors, or the evolution of business. Despite their already achieved success, the time spent learning about ways to improve both themselves and their business(es) is extensive.

Yet this makes perfect sense. Of course, the most successful entrepreneurs will be those who are always one step ahead of the competition, improving the quality of the product that they are providing, or thinking ahead into the future. If they did not continually look for ways to improve, they will be overtaken by competition, from businesses run by entrepreneurs who are using this characteristic, and reaping the benefits.

In Richard Branson's autobiography, he stated how despite the heights of entrepreneurial success he has reached, "I still have a hell of a lot to learn", and that "I will continue questioning, questioning, questioning". This suggests how the characteristic of continuously learning and improving comes almost naturally to him. He went on to say how "I consider myself a good listener, and apportion a good deal of my success to this". Again, this emphasizes just how fundamental it is to always be learning and improving.

There is no better evidence of Branson having this characteristic than the fact that he has a mentor. Richard Branson, in control of over 500 companies generating over $20 billion in annual revenue, has a mentor! One of the most successful entrepreneurs on earth has still, after all those billions, the desire and willingness to learn and improve. and it is that same characteristic which has enabled him to get to the position he is in today. With an unrelenting hunger for learning and improving, he has been able to outsmart competition and fully understand the faults in his businesses.

Henry Ford's story proved how the keen desire to learn helped lead him to success. After realising the potential of the newly developed gas engine, he recognised that he needed to learn about the basics of electricity, as the gas engine was fired by an electric spark. In order to figure out how it functioned, he committed the next three years of his life to work in the 'Edison Alluminating Factory', a company in Detroit which produced electricity for the local area. This way, he could then apply this new-found knowledge to his own work, which eventually gained him a lot of success.

John Roberts is always listening to podcasts. When driving somewhere, he will often put on a podcast relevant to business or entrepreneurial development. Despite running a successful business with over fifty employees, he is continuously learning from podcasts in order to improve himself as an entrepreneur. He even listens to some of the podcast at 1.5 times the speed, so that he can absorb more information in a shorter space of time! Imagine there is an competitive entrepreneur in the same industry as John, who never seeks to improve himself by reading or listening to podcasts. All the while John is listening to his podcasts and gaining information from them, is time that the other entrepreneur is not. This extra useful information can therefore give John the edge over his competitors. His inquisitive nature and desire to improve is one of the main reasons why he is a successful entrepreneur.

Another entrepreneur who strongly showed this as a characteristic is Mark Cuban. After selling his first business, 'MicroSolutions' for $6 million in 1990, he spent years learning as much as he possible could about the internet and its potential, and how he could profit from the way it was going to revolutionise society. This led to the creation of 'Broadcast.com' which he later sold for $6 billion this time. Many people would have relaxed after receiving $6 million, many would have retired, but Cuban's desire to continually learn after reaching success enabled him to become one of the richest men in America. Nowadays, this characteristic of his is still in full force. He is currently concerned with Artificial Intelligence how it is going to reshape the way we live, so trying to learn as much as he can about it. He will therefore be able to understand how it is going to affect his business, and whether it may prove to be a threat. Likewise, by learning about it before his competitors do, he may be able to use it to his advantage. He has even taken online classes on the subject, and has bought a book named 'AI for Dummies'![xxii]

The desire and the willingness to constantly and consistently learn is a characteristic which has been key in the story of many successful entrepreneurs. Having a never-ending curiosity and enthusiasm to improve will be with many of these entrepreneurs forever, and is one of the main reasons why the most successful entrepreneurs find themselves having achieved their goals and reached success. Do you have this characteristic, are you working as hard to constantly learn and improve as your competitors?

Being a skilled salesperson

The third most important characteristic of successful entrepreneurs is the ability of skilled salesmanship. Salesmanship is defined as 'the skills and methods used in selling or promoting commercial products' This is the characteristic behind every successful entrepreneur, and there is a directly proportional link between the ability that the entrepreneur has to sell, and the success of the business. At the end of the day, business is all about selling something to someone else, so being skilled at selling the product or service concerned usually determines how successful the business will be.

For entrepreneurs, salesmanship is involved in every aspect of a business. Not only is it the crucial factor in the selling of a good or service, but it is also used for convincing investors to invest, for convincing critical employees to join or stay etc. It is the overall impact of being a good salesperson that gives it such importance in the makings of a successful entrepreneur.

Being a good salesperson is commonly confused with being very persuasive. Although persuasion is most definitely a factor when it comes to salesmanship, there is much more to being a good salesman than being a good persuader. Persuasion refers to convincing someone to do something, usually against their will, whereas honest salesmanship involves trust, a genuine connection between the seller and the buyer, and a solid belief in the good being sold.

Although many of the entrepreneurs that I have researched believe they have been given the natural talent of salesmanship, I believe it is entirely possible to be able to gain it through practise.

Many of the successful entrepreneurs involved in my research have shown signs of being a skilled salesman from a young age. In an article written about the life of Mark Cuban, he was described as displaying a "tenacity for making a deal and carving out a better life for himself". He also described how "I found out early that I was a good salesperson", and went on to say; "as long as I can remember I was buying and selling baseball cards, garbage bags, whatever I could find". This trait of being a naturally gifted salesman has been carried through his life, and has played such an influential role in the success of the many companies he has since built.

Likewise, Richard Branson acquired the characteristic of being a skilled salesman at a young age. At only 16, he had founded 'Student Magazine', and by twenty years of age had his own record shop on Oxford Street. Again, this natural talent for salesmanship proved its weight in gold throughout his career. His work with the 'Virgin Group' involved constantly selling ideas to investors. He managed to secure a $100 million investment from Abu Dhabi for the development of Virgin Galactic back in 2009, and explained in his biography just how important the ability to sell was when negotiating the deal. He said, "The key is to display passion, know-how and determination." Having the natural ability to sell has been influential in Branson's success, without it he would never have been able to secure the investments which have helped the Virgin brand achieve its status today.

Even in my short experience of entrepreneurship, I have been exposed to the importance of being a good salesperson. On many occasions, I have had to sell the idea of buying a bubble waffle to onlookers, who are initially unsure. By smiling, appearing inviting and having confidence in the product I am selling, I have managed to convince many to by a waffle, who would otherwise have simply walked away. Although I believe it is too early to consider myself as a hugely successful entrepreneur, I have realised the importance and necessity of being a good salesperson, and the great potential it brings with it.

John and Paul both worked in sales before becoming entrepreneurs. John worked for a company selling engineering tools, while Paul was selling commercial refrigeration. When speaking to them, they both explained how the skills and subtle tricks they learnt during their time as salesmen were priceless, and played such an instrumental role in the success of their businesses. Their prior ability to sell meant that attracting customers to do business with came as second nature, and it was the management and maintenance side of the company that in fact came much less naturally for them.

No matter the industry, your ability to sell will be a defining factor in the success of your business. Being a skilled salesperson will make attracting customers and employees so much easier, whereas lacking the ability to sell to will make building and running a business nigh-on impossible.

Key takeaways from this section:

- Resilience is the characteristic most important to entrepreneurial success, it enables you to recover strongly when things go wrong, and maintains a sustained work ethic until success is reached.
- The desire to continuously learn and improve enables you to always stay one step ahead of your competition and allows you to more accurately predict the future of a business and an industry.
- The ability to sell is key for an entrepreneur; it is required to gain customers and investment, and attract and retain key employees.

Louis Callaghan-Inge

Conclusion

This guidebook has now provided you with information about the characteristics of a successful entrepreneur. You have understood what success means to entrepreneurs, how entrepreneurs gain the characteristics which lead them to success, how the characteristics of a successful entrepreneur have changed over time, and finally the three most important characteristics themselves.

Implementing the characteristics outlined in this short guide into your own character will take time. Don't expect to wake up tomorrow and suddenly be a genius salesman, or with an overwhelming desire to learn about the industry you are in. But over time, practising these characteristics will make them second nature, and you will start to see the reward they bring.

Although the characteristics which entrepreneurs possess are key to their success, there are undoubtedly many more factors. The characteristics of an entrepreneur are the building blocks of how they think and behave, however matters such as the quality of the product that the entrepreneur is selling, their relations between staff, decision making at key times, management style etc are all components which influence the extent of the entrepreneur's success. Even with the most optimal combination of characteristics, an entrepreneur may still fail due to these other factors.

That being said, applying the advice provided from this book will no doubt increase your chance of reaching success as an entrepreneur. There is no more fool-proof method of achieving success than following in the footsteps of those who have been before. Failure to apply the characteristics explained in this book will almost certainly lead to failure. Having the characteristics of a successful entrepreneur, self-belief and a touch of luck, will no doubt result in prosperity.

As the Great Richard Branson wrote "It is entrepreneurs who have the potential to change the world." Successful entrepreneurs will continue to innovate, excite and improve the way we live our lives, whilst profiting in the process. Are you going be one of them?

Acknowledgements

I would like to say a special thank you to both John Roberts and Paul Thomas for their time, and for sharing their experience and wisdom. The information they both provided wasn't just vital in the creation of this book, but will undoubtedly be used by me in whatever entrepreneurial ventures I may pursue in the future.

A Guide to the Characteristics of the Successful

References

[ii] Richard Branson, Finding My Virginity, 2017
[iii] Definition of a characteristic from Oxford Languages
[iv] Biography.com, Henry Ford Biography, 2014
[v] Definition of philanthropism from Oxford Languages
[vi] Yahoo Finance, YouTube.com, 2019
[vii] Gordon Allport, Trait Theory, 1936
[viii] Personality Questionnaire, Hans Eysenck, 1975
[ix] Biography.com, Henry Ford Biography, 2014
[x] Suliman Taeb, J.P Morgan, myhero.com, 2018
[xi] Albert Bandura, Social Learning Theory, 1977
[xii] Albert Bandura, Bobo Doll experiment, 1961
[xiii] Hollander, Interactionist approach, 1967
[xiv] buisinessalligators.com, 11 personality traits of Henry Ford, 2016
[xv] Henry Ford, My Life and Work, 1922
[xvi] Business Casual, Youtube.com, 2019
[xvii] Wikipedia.com, Robber Baron article
[xviii] Real-Insight-Network.com, WBD study, 2019
[xix] Jessie Connor, Mystartupland.com, 2019
[xx] Valuetainement, YouTube.com, 2018
[xxi] Carayannis and Stewart, Obsessed maniacs and clairvoyant oracles, 2013
[xxii] John Paul Mueller, AI for dummies, 2018

Front cover designed by Louis Callaghan-Inge

www.ingramcontent.com/pod-product-compliance
Lightning Source LLC
Chambersburg PA
CBHW070812220526
45466CB00002B/643